the log in my eye

double-act sketches
with a message

Michael Catchpool and Pat Lunt

Kevin
Mayhew

First published in 1998 by
KEVIN MAYHEW LTD
Rattlesden
Bury St Edmunds
Suffolk IP30 0SZ

0 1 2 3 4 5 6 7 8 9

ISBN 1 84003 194 8
Catalogue No 1500207

Cover illustration: *Faces II* by Diana Ong
Reproduced courtesy of SuperStock, London
Cover design by Jaquetta Sargeant

Edited by David Gatward
Typesetting by Louise Selfe
Printed in Great Britain

Contents

Acknowledgements

Thanks are due to everybody who has asked us to write and perform the sketches included in this book for their encouragement and support. Thanks also to all those who have shared the laughter with us and to our wives and families who have put up with us disappearing for hours on end to write, and endured all the silly voices while we rehearsed. A special thanks, too, to everybody who ever said, 'You really ought to write those sketches down!'

About the Authors

Catchpool (Michael) is coming to terms with looking at 'the wrong side of 30'. He is a Deputy Headteacher at a junior school and is married with two children. He went to Oxford (once, for a day-trip) and has a postcard to prove it. Michael has had no experience as a veterinary surgeon, but he does have a degree in drama.

Lunt (Pat) has long forgotten what it was like coming to terms with looking at 'the wrong side of 30', and wonders what Catchpool (Michael) is making all the fuss about. He is married, with one daughter, and is a teacher at a local school. He has never ski-ed down the east face of Mount Kilimanjaro, but has been up to London several times on a bus.

Catchpool and Lunt have been writing and performing together for a number of years. They have performed their material in many venues (and survived each occasion). They also perform frequently on both commercial and local BBC radio.

Introduction

Picture, if you will, the scene inside an exclusive luncheon club. (Go on, use your imagination.*) You can hear the distinctive tinkle of lead crystal glasses as fine vintage wine is poured, and there is the unmistakable sound of sophisticated chatter and badinage over the *hors d'oeuvres*. But wait, all is not well over by the salmon and asparagus vol-au-vents. There appears to be a slight altercation between long-standing member Colonel Sir General Duke Charles Fortesque Smythe and a newcomer . . .

Colonel   I say, my man! I can't believe they've let you in here dressed like that. It's an outrage! Where's your tie, man? You're letting the side down terribly. Certainly no way to appear in public! Have you no standards? No sense of common decency? No understanding of what's right and wrong? Of what sets us apart from the animals? I say to you again, sir – where is your tie?

Newcomer   And I say to you, sir – where are your trousers?

             (*Exeunt et al – not pursued by bear*)

Could it happen? Surely not? Who would be so judgemental when they have such obvious faults themselves? We wouldn't . . . but then again . . .

It's very easy to see just what's wrong with everybody else. Like an aged doctor, who nods sagely and says, 'Well, you see, you've got a nasty bout of . . .', or, 'It wouldn't surprise me if you didn't have a case of the . . .', and then with a quick, illegible scribble on a pad, prescribes just the medicine they think is needed.

We, as Christians, or even as the Church, can be the same. The temptation is often so very hard to resist. We can be caught nodding and saying such things as, 'You see, you've got a nasty habit of . . .', or, 'It wouldn't surprise me if you didn't need to . . .' And then we think of just the right prescription to make those people much more the way we feel they ought to be.

The trouble is that every now and then what we really need is a bit of a nudge to topple us from our soap boxes and for someone to drag us (preferably not by the ears) to a mirror and in subtle tones say, 'Hang on a minute! But what about the log in your own eye?'

---

*If you do not need to use your imagination, then you are obviously a member of such a club – could you recommend us for membership?

The sketches and thoughts in this book give just that opportunity to gaze in the mirror and to begin to realise that it's not just others who need to have a little think. All manner of topics are considered from 'prayer' to 'paradise' and from 'firefighting' to 'How should you build a tower anyway?'

You know, as Shakespeare never once said, 'Drama can be sneaky. One moment we think we're laughing at how ridiculous other people can be and the next we can find that we are laughing at ourselves and our own ridiculous way of going about things in the Church and in our own Christian life.'

And it is in the protection of this laughter that we, as individuals and as a Church, may just feel bold enough to do something about what's lurking in our own eye, so that we can develop and grow and be less concerned with the speck in someone else's.

So, a meaningful sketch with just two performers . . . Is it possible? Of course it is! These sketches are written especially for two willing (?) volunteers. All require little or no extra props or costume. No previous experience required . . . just a bit of enthusiasm!

Emergency 999

Sometimes we are very aware of the need for help in our lives . . . and sometimes it takes an emergency for us to realise. But if we want Christ to do something in our lives, are we going to allow him in to deal with everything, or are there some areas we feel are strictly off limits?

Characters   Maud: an old, nervy and excitable woman.
Fireman: businesslike and keen to do his job.

(*Maud is on stage, pacing nervously up and down*)

Maud   (*Greatly agitated*) Oooh . . . Ooooooh!

Fireman   (*Enters as if carrying fire-fighting hose and making fire-engine noises*) Nee-naw-nee-naw-nee-naw . . . Never fear, your friendly fireman is here!

Maud   (*Ecstatically*) Oh you're here, I'm saved! Oh wonderful! Oh super! Oh marvellous! Oh . . . sit down and have a cup of tea.

Fireman   Well, thanks very much. (*He sits, relaxes momentarily, then jumps up, remembering why he has come*) No! No! There's a fire! (*He begins to make a move to look for the fire. Then* **Maud** *gently restrains him*)

Maud   Oh now don't you worry about that, dear . . .

Fireman   But I must . . . It's my job. I've got to put the fire out. I'll start in here . . . (*He moves off again and is again restrained*)

Maud   (*Alarmed*) No!

Fireman   What?

Maud	Oh no . . . you can't go in there . . . No, I haven't dusted in there yet; the place is a terrible mess. I don't want you thinking I live in a pig-sty.
Fireman	But I must, madam . . . the fire!
Maud	No!
Fireman	(*Turns and tries to make off in another direction*) Well I'll go in here then . . .
Maud	(*Restraining the fireman*) No!
Fireman	(*Exasperated*) What?
Maud	Oh no, you can't go in there.
Fireman	Why ever not?
Maud	(*Whispers her reasons to the fireman*)
Fireman	(*Reacting as if a little shocked*) Really?
Maud	(*She nods, somewhat shamefaced. She whispers some more revelations*)
Fireman	(*In disbelief*) Three weeks!?
Maud	(*Ashamedly*) Hmmm.
Fireman	(*Deciding he can handle it*) Never mind, I've seen dirty washing before . . .
Maud	Well you're not seeing mine!
Fireman	Well how about in here then? (*Making a move in another direction*)
Maud	Oooh no!
Fireman	What?
Maud	Oh no . . . We don't go in there!

Fireman	Why not?
Maud	Well . . . I had an argument with my sister Enid; Christmas 1953 it was . . . I've not forgiven her . . . we've not been in there since.
Fireman	But madam, your house is on fire!
Maud	(*Continuing to ramble about the argument with her sister*) And when I think of some of the hurtful things she said, I mean, I couldn't believe it at the time . . .
Fireman	(*Trying to get* **Maud's** *attention*) Your house is on fire!
Maud	(*Still rambling*) . . . and I can't believe it now. I mean, I know she said that I'd said some terrible things to her but I think I was just being honest and if people can't take a bit of honesty when it's given with the best inten . . .
Fireman	(*Loudly*) Your house is on fire!
Maud	(*Annoyed*) I know my house is on fire. You haven't got to tell me my house is on fire. That's why I called you . . . I don't know, put a hose in their hand, a hat on their head and they think they're mastermind or something . . . Coming in here telling me my house is on fire . . . whatever next? Must think I'm stupid . . .
Fireman	(*After a pronounced intake of breath*) Right. Well I'll start upstairs then. (*He begins to move off*)
Maud	(*Shocked*) Ooh no! You can't go in there. That's where I keep all me . . . all me nick-nacks.
Fireman	(*Incredulously*) Your nick-nacks?
Maud	Yes . . . I can't have you going upstairs lookin' at my nick-nacks. I mean . . . what would the neighbours say?

Fireman	But I wouldn't be looking at your nick-nacks. I'd be putting out the fire.
Maud	Oh no . . . It wouldn't be right.
Fireman	Well, where *can* I go? I can't go in there because you haven't dusted . . . I can't go in there because of your . . . (*Leans over and whispers*)
Maud	(*A little embarrassed*) Hmmm.
Fireman	I can't go in there because you had an argument with your sister . . . er . . . (*trying to remember the name*)
Maud	Enid.
Fireman	Enid, that's it. And I can't go in there because of your nick-nacks.
Maud	Well . . . the neighbours would be . . . you know?
Fireman	So, madam, where *can* I go?
Maud	Well, can't you just squirt it around a bit in here? (*She gestures to suggest the immediate surroundings. The* **Fireman** *is eventually persuaded to go along with this and does so half-heartedly*) There now. That wasn't so bad was it? Now you just sit down and I'll put the kettle on . . . and I've got a nice plate of macaroons – home-made mind you, none of this . . . (*She stops herself mid-sentence and points. Then speaks rather agitatedly*) Ooh! What's that?
Fireman	Where?
Maud	(*Still pointing*) There!
Fireman	(*Looking where she indicates. He sees what he has expected to see and with controlled patience explains*) Ah, well, those are flames, madam.
Maud	What? And those there? (*Points to another place*)

Fireman	Yes, they're flames as well.
Maud	And those? (*Pointing to another place*)
Fireman	Yes, they're all flames.
Maud	And what's that, billowing down the stairs?
Fireman	(*Considering a good description*) Um . . . Heavy smoke, madam . . . and more flames if I'm not too much mistaken.
Maud	(*Although the fireman seems almost resigned to the fact that the situation is out of control,* **Maud** *now begins to become a little hysterical*) Oh look, they're everywhere . . . There! There! There! Oh *do* something! *Do* something! My house is burning down. Oh help . . . Why didn't you do anything? Why didn't you do anything to help me?
Fireman	Well . . . you wouldn't let me in!

END

There are many reasons why we keep parts of our lives locked away. It could be a painful memory, something sad that has happened, or something we just feel too embarrassed to share – it's just too private. Perhaps we feel that there are parts of our lives that aren't in order and we don't want to acknowledge them until they are more presentable. But when we invite Christ in, we are inviting in the person who knew all about us when we were in the womb; who knows the number of hairs on our head; who knows our every thought and the desires of our heart. And knowing us that intimately still – despite what we may think – hasn't put him off. In fact, he loves us beyond the point of death and wants to be able to help us deal with not just a part of our life but with all of it. Some of it we may be scared about. Some of it we may feel angry about. But Christ wants to be there . . . before we are overcome by smoke!

Simon – Swiftest Sword
this Side of Swindon

What's in a name? It's one thing to call yourself a Christian but what are some of the things it should involve? Well, perhaps a checklist that says, 'If you do all these then you're doing great!' isn't the way. But surely if we are serious, then being a Christian must involve things such as:

Spending time with God.

A desire to find out more about him.

Fellowship with others.

Being prepared to face the challenge of the enemy.

Eagerness, being prepared, ready for the challenge . . . Aren't these all the attributes of a Royal Musketeer, sir?

Characters   Simon: a musketeer by name but not much else.
Roderick: a brave and earnest fellow.

(**Roderick** *and* **Simon** *approach each other with a swagger and exchange exaggerated bows and greetings*)

Roderick   I bid thee good morn, sir.

Simon   And to you, sir, with a hey and a nonny.

Roderick   Well, a hey and a nonny nonny no to you, sir.

Simon   (*Not to be outdone*) And a hey and a nonny nonny no, with little twiddly bits to you.

Roderick   (*sensing that this could get ridiculous*) I thank thee for thy kind greeting. But pray, whom do I have the pleasure of addressing?

Simon   I, sir, am a musketeer; Simon – swiftest sword this side of Swindon.

Roderick   Then I am most honoured to meet thee, Simon – swiftest sword this side of Swindon, for I myself have pondered much upon becoming a musketeer. Oft-times have I heard of their bravery, their dedication to their cause and their loyalty to the king. (**Simon** *makes suitably puffed up and condescending gestures, fiddles with gauntlets, that sort of thing*) But Simon – swiftest sword this side of Swindon, may I prevail upon you as I seek answers to questions which have sore vexed my mind? (**Simon** *nods his permission*) Is the musketeer's life one of real dedication?

Simon   Why yes! For a musketeer must practise his sword skills every day like me, er . . . (*He begins to muse*) except for yesterday, because the weather wasn't too good, and the day before as well, come to that . . . In fact, come to think of it, I didn't get to do much sword-skill practising at all last week, what with friends coming round and one thing and another . . . still I have got some time pencilled in for next week . . . though that might clash with the gardening, if the weather picks up . . . but no matter, (*with emphasis*) for I am still a musketeer!

Roderick   Then Simon, tell me of your sword, for that must truly be a most formidable weapon.

Simon   Why yes! See where my rapier hangs. (*He looks down. There is an embarrassing pause as he sees there is nothing there. He makes a quick recovery and bluffs*) Rather, see where my rapier would have hung had I remembered it. Methinks it is by the fireplace where I was using it as a toasting fork. But still, I do have my dagger (*he reaches to where a dagger might be – there is nothing*) – no I don't . . . er . . . but I do have . . . (*fumbling through clothing, eventually finding something which is presented with a flourish*) . . . a toothpick! This will suffice, and no matter for I am still a musketeer!

Roderick   Strange weaponry indeed for a musketeer, do you not think, Simon – swiftest . . . toothpick this side of Swindon? But pray, tell me of the fine musketeer's garb.

Simon   Why yes! The musketeer's garb . . . (*He looks at his own rather ordinary clothes*) Actually, methinks mine is in the potting shed . . . for the plumed hat is most useful for carrying my seed potatoes hither and thither . . . and the cape is good to kneel upon when one is weeding or planting . . . Zounds! I am remembered of my dagger – it too is in the garden for it makes an excellent dibber – to make the holes for my seed potatoes you understand . . . But no matter, for I am still a musketeer!

Roderick   (*Looking a little bewildered during the last speech but still persisting*) Simon – swiftest toothpick this side of Swindon, I am most envious of you, for you must spend much time communing with the king.

Simon   (*Beginning to feel a bit shaky*) Well yes . . . or rather, no . . . I met often with the king when I first became a musketeer but now, well you know how things are? (*trails off, thinking*) . . . the other musketeers seem to spend a lot of time communing with the king but, to tell you the truth, I don't seem to be able to find the time.

Roderick   Too much carousing I'll be bound, eh, Simon? You and your fellow musketeers meeting together, that must be an exciting revel!

Simon   Ah, yes . . . the carousing . . . No, I don't get to do much carousing with the other musketeers, not now. I'm a bit of a loner I suppose . . . like to keep myself to myself . . . none of the others seem to be that interested in gardening either, I'm afraid . . .

Always say they're too busy on the king's business. But no matter, for I am still a musketeer!

Roderick   Then Simon – swiftest toothpick this side of Swindon, pray tell me, if you will, of your frays with the enemy, for they must be a great challenge for you?

Simon   Well, actually, I try not to get involved. I don't like poking my nose in . . . you know. Anyway, I don't seem to have much time for that just now, I mean the garden won't weed itself . . .

Roderick   But soft, (*He turns to listen*) what is that noise, Simon?

Simon   Oh, I'm sorry, I had beans for tea.

Roderick   No, not that noise . . . that noise . . .

Simon   (*Guessing*) Sounds like thunder.

Roderick   No, (*excitedly*) 'tis mounted horse; ten – maybe twenty!

Simon   Really, how clever of you ! I don't think I could have recognised that.

Roderick   Perchance it is the enemy, pressing in hard upon us in this dark, foreboding wood!

Simon   (*Horrified*) The enemy – pressing in hard upon us in this dark, foreboding wood!

Roderick   We must prepare!

Simon   (*Hopefully*) Prepare to run away?

Roderick   No, sir, prepare to fight!

Simon	I don't think that's really necessary, is it?
Roderick	Too late, for they are upon us! (*A mimed fight ensues with* **Roderick** *bravely slicing away while* **Simon** *cowers in various places, occasionally popping up to make a pathetic jab with his toothpick*) Dare to cross swords with me, sir! Why then, you shall soon taste my cold steel. Take that! And that! (*To* **Simon**) How goes it with you, Simon – swiftest toothpick this side of Swindon?
Simon	(*Rather quietly*) Er . . . not very well really . . .
Roderick	(*Still thrusting away at the enemy*) Take that, sir! Have at you! . . . You scoundrel . . . Take that! See, Simon, they are running . . . like mongrel dogs with their tails between their legs! See how they flee, we are victorious. (*He turns to find* **Simon** *kneeling, cowering on the floor*) Simon . . . how goes it, sir? . . . your toothpick? . . . Methought you said you were a musketeer and yet in truth, it would seem you are a musketeer more in name, sir, than in action. (**Roderick** *helps Simon to his feet and they exit*)

END

The honour, the adventure, the privilege, the challenge of being a musketeer . . . one of the king's chosen . . . and Simon has messed it all up. And his claim, 'But I am still a musketeer!' begins to have a hollow ring. When he is finally challenged his response was sadly predictable and inevitable.

If we say we are Christian, how is that shown? What effect does it have? What commitments have we made to the challenges. Or is there a hollow ring to our claims?

A Course on Prayer

50p in the slot and out comes the chocolate; if you put something in, you expect something out. Which is the sort of attitude we can have to prayer. You put the right words and phrases in and something good is bound to come out the other end. Well surely that's our right as consumers?

THE SKETCH

(One performer moves to centre stage or we hear the announcement from offstage)

Announcer This is an Open University programme. Religious Education, Module Three, Section Seven, Programme 1: The Four Stages of Prayer. Stage One: 'Vending Machine Prayer'.

Lesson 1

Characters 1: A rather 'grey' fellow; a bit boring.

2: Another of the same type.

(**1** *and* **2** *sit, as if in a car, one driving, the other a passenger*)

1 Well, nearly there then.

2 Yes, I suppose it's nearly time.

1 Might as well make a start then.

2 Yes.

1 *(After a moment's silence, draws in a deep breath before continuing rather slowly and deliberately)* Oh Lord, as we approach the busy, bustling city centre, we come before you and humbly ask that out of your great bounty you might provide for us . . . a parking space.

2 Yes, Lord, and in the fullness of thy bounty we would ask not just for a half-hour parking but for the full two hours free parking, Lord.

1 Within easy level walking distance to the shops we hope to visit this afternoon.

2 Amen.

1 Amen.

(*They drive around for a while, keenly watching for the parking space. A stylised sequence of movements could be used here*)

2 Well, it's been half an hour, Lord, and we still have not found the parking space that you have provided for us . . .

1 Open our eyes, Lord, that we may see the parking space.

2 Yes, Lord, we claim that parking space in your name. Satan has no authority over that parking space, Lord.

1 Amen.

2 Amen.

(*Another period of driving follows. Repeating the same moves perhaps*)

1 Well, it's been an hour now, Lord, and we're running rather low on petrol.

2 Forgive us our lack of discernment, Lord, for we have not, as yet, found the parking space you have saved for us.

1 Yes, Lord, increase our sensitivity to your Spirit's leading.

2 Amen.

1 Amen.

(*After a short while it is apparent that the car has stopped (run out of petrol). In response, 1 and 2 are seen to get on a bus. They are now seated on the bus, still travelling. A series of stylised movements could be used to convey this*)

1 Well, Lord, we thank you for bringing along the Number 17 bus, only 45 minutes after we had run out of petrol on the outskirts of the city.

2 Thank you too that we were able to experience once again the wonder and power of your creation in the form of that freak thunderstorm and heavy downpour that caught us so totally unawares.

1 Amen.

2 Amen.

End of Lesson 1

We can sometimes see God as some giant vending machine. After we've said the right phrase, God is bound to provide us with what we want . . . no matter how trivial. 'Parking spaces within easy walking of the shops . . .' Of course God is interested in all aspects of our lives but we must be careful that our prayer doesn't become selfish, or trivial and thereby trivialise prayer and God.

Lesson 2

'Good sir, I desire to procure from you a variety of items in exchange for a fixed monetary sum, in a manner which will be beneficial to both parties.'

We wouldn't ask for a newspaper and a tin of cat food at the local shop like that, but we can sometimes use the most extraordinary language, not with strangers but with someone who's known us all our lives. Strange really!

Characters   1: A verbose and somewhat long-winded person.

             2: A concise translator.

(One performer moves to centre stage or we hear the announcement from offstage)

Announcer Lesson Number 2: 'Prayer – an exercise in translation.'

(The two performers stand slightly apart. The first says the prayers with an over-the-top, theatrical delivery. The second in a very ordinary style – more genuine perhaps?)

1 Oh most omnipotent Lord, God of hosts, King of kings, I come before thee knowing that I have transgressed and fallen short of thy most perfect ways.

2 Oh God . . . I messed up.

1 Why, my failings are as black as the night and are as like unto the stainings of soot upon the new-fallen snow.

2 I really messed up!

1 Oh what a vile instrument is the tongue, for though it is such a small thing it acts like the rudder of a great ship turning it this way and that, often into dangerous waters.

19

2 I swore.

1 And what instruments of pain and discomfort can be the hands and feet of men that do mete out such evil and pain upon our fellow creatures.

2 I kicked the cat.

1 Turn me from my transgressions that I may step once more along thy righteous paths.

2 Help me not to do it again.

1 Amen.

2 Amen.

End of Lesson 2

Where do we get the idea that there is a set language for prayer? The only thing that is set is the need to be genuine and honest.

Lesson 3

So there's something you need to say to someone. It's been nagging away at you for ages. So when's the best time to say it? Well surely that's obvious . . . at a prayer meeting!

Characters 1: A friendly and welcoming prayer meeting leader.

2: A person with 'a bit of an axe to grind'.

(One performer moves to centre stage or we hear the announcement from offstage)

Announcer: Lesson Number 3: 'Horizontal Prayer'.

(The two figures sit, as if at a prayer meeting)

1 Well, I'm glad that we could all gather for this prayer meeting. And if anyone has anything that they have on their hearts, then do share it now in prayer, as the Spirit leads . . .

(Throughout the following prayer 1 looks increasingly uneasy and unsettled. There are a few moments of silence)

2 *(Forcefully)* Well, I believe tonight the Lord wants to speak particularly to those people who may have borrowed something from other people and have forgotten to return it. Lay a burden, Lord, on the hearts of those who have borrowed, perhaps, gardening equipment – which they may have left lurking in the shed or propped up behind the greenhouse despite specific requests that such equipment not be left out, open to the elements or the light-fingered touch of thieves and vagabonds. Lord, open their eyes to the considerable inconvenience and misery they are causing their brother who is unable to do a number of small but important jobs around his own garden until such equipment is returned. Amen.

1 Ah . . . er . . . (*Quietly and a bit awkwardly*) Amen.

End of Lesson 3

Prayer is a way of drawing close to God. Enjoying the chance to communicate with him. And we can share that experience with others but when we bring our own petty agendas along, our prayers can just become words that far from travelling vertically, take a much more horizontal route. Is this really what praying together is really all about?

Lesson 4

Ask an honest question, get an honest answer. But sometimes an honest answer is the last thing we want to hear . . . bit too much of a challenge. Still, we can always pray about it!

Characters 1: A rather gushing and 'terribly well-meaning' person.

2: A person experiencing unfortunate circumstances.

(*One performer moves to centre stage or we hear the announcement from offstage*)

Announcer Lesson Number 4: 'Supportive Prayer'.

(*The two performers approach from opposite sides of the stage. 1 opens with a typical breezy greeting*)

1 Hello! How are you?

2 (*Being honest. Subdued*) Oh . . . not too good really. Well, pretty awful actually. I've lost my job. Things are very tense at home and it's affecting the kids badly. It's like my whole world is sort of crumbling down around me.

1   (*Having looked momentarily unnerved by these honest revelations, quickly recovers to offer . . .*) Well, shall we have a little talk to Jesus?

2   (*Slightly confused*) You mean, pray?

1   Yes, that's right.

2   Some prayer would be really good, yeah . . .

1   Good . . . (*Warming to their theme*) Oh, Lord, we thank you for all the lovely things we see around us. The lovely trees and the pretty flowers. The lovely scent as the warm breeze blows across their petals. For the lovely song of the birds that cheers us in the mornings as the golden sun peeps over the hills to spread its glorious light and warmth over all that you have made. Lord, you have given us so much for which we can be thankful and we thank you for them all now. Amen . . . (*Turning to* 2) Now then, feeling better?

2   (*Probably even more despondent*) Er . . . yeah . . . great.

End of Lesson 4

Announcer   That was an Open University programme, Religious Education, Module Three, Section Seven. The next programme in this series deals with 'Baptism for Beginners' and considers aspects such as 'How to hold a baby without dropping it', and 'Are water wings acceptable attire for total-immersion baptism?'

Supportive prayer is about responding to the real needs and worries of the individual, however challenging that might be. It may not be comfortable, but then we need to be prepared to stop thinking about ourselves so that our prayer becomes genuine, realistic and relevant.

The Cake Appreciation Society

Are we as welcoming as we think? Because there's 'welcoming' and then there's 'welcoming'. How often are people put off by us, the church, wanting them to fit our mould rather than us accepting them as individuals and all they have to offer? Is church a flexible, comfortable place of acceptance or an archaic, rigid institution that is more concerned with tradition and new pipes for the organ than with the needs of the individuals who find their way inside?

Jesus said simply, 'Follow me', not, 'Put on your best clothes, shine your shoes, say the right things and follow me'.

Characters   The President of the Cake Appreciation Society: a pompous and wordy person.
A Visitor (with his right arm in a sling).

(*We see the imposing figure of the* **President** *standing behind a lectern. The* **Visitor** *to the Society is seated to one side*)

President   (*In a grandiose manner, as if reading from speech notes*) Well, a warm welcome to you all to the Cake Appreciation Society, and a particularly warm welcome to any visitors with us today. *(Nods smilingly in the direction of the visitor)* And as we do have some new faces among us, it gives us a good opportunity to reflect once again on the interesting history of the Cake Appreciation Society. (*Pause. Deep breath*) It was as far back as 1535 when the great Cecil de Maundeville first stated his wish that, 'All should enjoy the pleasure of eating cake and benefit thus from its nourishment and wholesome nature.' But it was not until 1662 and the famous Battenburg Committee, led by the distinguished Dr William Peeps, that the Cake Appreciation Society really took shape. It was this committee that provided us with what some may argue are the most important guidelines that give the Cake Appreciation Society its distinctive approach.

And so, in the manner which the Battenburg Committee and the distinguished Dr. William Peeps devised, let us prepare to eat the cakes. Visitors, you are most welcome to join us. So now, as always, since 1662, let us take the cake with our right hand, from the plate on our right-hand side, and lift it to our mouths and enjoy the nourishment and wholesome nature thereof. Together, with the right hand we reach, taking from the right . . . (*Through the last part of this speech, the* **Visitor** *has been trying to attract the attention of the* **President**, *pointing to his sling, to make his predicament obvious*)

Visitor	(*Raising left arm*) Um . . . excuse me . . .
President	(*Rather impatiently*) Yes?
Visitor	Um, sorry to interrupt . . . er, bit of a problem.
President	What?
Visitor	With that bit just near the beginning . . . could you just go back a bit . . . Would you mind terribly?
President	(*Heavy sigh*) Right . . . (*Mechanically*) Let us take the cake with our right hand, from the plate on our right-hand side . . .
Visitor	(*Interrupting*) Yes, that's it! That's the bit! Now I don't want to be a nuisance, and lots of what's been said, I love. You see I love the plate. The cake on the plate . . . I love. But where you've got me, er . . . stymied, so to speak, is the 'take with your right hand' bit. That's the stumbling block for me here, and I'd very much like to enjoy the pleasure of eating the cake, and the wholesome nature an' that . . . so I was wondering would anyone mind if I used my left hand?

President   (*Loudly*) Can you be serious, sir? Would you fly in the face of the important rulings of the famous Battenburg Committee of 1662 and the distinguished Dr William Peeps?

Visitor   Well it would make things a lot easier for me if I could, yes.

President   (*Affronted*) I daresay you think it would, sir! But I, for one, will not see centuries of tradition tossed aside for the mere trifle of your convenience. We are not a charity, sir! We are a Cake Appreciation Society!

Visitor   And I appreciate that. No pun intended. But what appealed to me, y'see . . . what I liked was the words there of Cecil de Maundevillle, way back in 1535 wasn't it, 'All should enjoy the pleasure of eating cake, and benefit thus from its nourishment and wholesome nature.'

President   I know those words, sir! But I am concerned with the Battenburg Committee of 1662 and the distinguished Dr William Peeps. Without them we shall have anarchy!

Visitor   Yes, but with them I don't get any cake!

President   (*Crossly*) Do you bandy words with me, sir?

Visitor   Well, I'd rather have a piece of cake. If I could just use my left hand.

President   I cannot allow you, sir, to ignore the wise guidance of the Battenburg Committee of 1662. No sir, I will not have it.

Visitor   Well, it doesn't look as though I shall be having it either. Which is a pity, because, as I said, I was very taken with Cecil de Maundeville there, and his

	philosophy, you know, about how 'All should enjoy the pleasure of eating cakes' . . .
President	(*Passionately*) Tradition, sir, tradition. It is what sets us apart from the animals. And it is that tradition that has been handed down to us from th . . .
Visitor	(*Interrupting.*) Yes, don't tell me. From the Battenburg Committee of 1662 and the distinguished, and – I've no doubt – uninjured and unencumbered Dr William bloomin' Peeps. (*Stands*) Right, well I think I'll be off then. I can't say that the Cake Appreciation Society does much for me. (*Slowly exits*)
President	(*Calling after him*) Well, sir, it will be a shame to see you leave us, but if you feel you must . . . (*Addressing the rest of the meeting*) Next week we meet again and do encourage your friends to come along . . .
Visitor	(*Shouting from the back*) Yeah, if they haven't broken their arm.
President	(*Spluttering coughs to try and cover up this embarrassing display*) Er, yes. Thank you for coming. (*He looks around, then down at the cake*) Well . . . if no one wants that cake. (*He moves over to the cake and pops it into his mouth. Exits with mouth full of cake*)

END

Have we the 'Cake Appreciation Society' mentality? 'Do as we do; if you don't, don't do it here because we don't want you to do your thing your way while we're doing our thing our way.'

Are we imposing a model of 'Church' as we understand it or genuinely communicating the Gospel of Christ?

Fire! . . . Fire! . . . Fire!

Out of the mouths of babes and sucklings comes all manner of things. A lot of it needs to be wiped away with a bib but sometimes it is words to which we should be listening. Too quickly we can dismiss what young people have to say. How easy and arrogant it is to say, 'The youth are the church of tomorrow'. (Don't let them bother us today.)

Young people are and should be very much a part of the church now. They are an integral part of the body of Christ, with important, relevant and challenging things to offer. So then, if you have ears . . .

Characters   Father: a rather stressed, unsympathetic chap.
                    Son: a young child, a little nervous.

(**Father** *is alone on stage, talking to an unseen listener*)

Father   Oh I know, because well, he told me the same thing – exactly the same thing. And that was only yesterday and I was shocked, well I say I was shocked but only part of me. Yes, part of me was surprised because I . . . (*etc. – ad lib in a similar manner*)

Child   (*Enters at a bit of a rush*) Daddy! . . . Daddy!

Father   (*To* **Child**) Er – not just now, I'm talking. (*To listener*) Well, yes, as you were saying, that's true, what you were saying, but then again that's not the first time is it? . . . Is it? That many times! Well, I wouldn't have thought that . . .

Child   But it's very important.

Father   Yes, well I don't think it's going to be as important as what Daddy has to say. Now be quiet and I might buy you an ice-cream. (*To listener*) Anyway, the funny thing is, the last time I saw him it was two – or could it be three – no couldn't be – that long ago, really? Well, one moment it's there and the next moment it's gone.

Child Daddy, it's just that if you don't do something about the present situation I think you might find yourself in a very awkward predicament.

Father (*After a moment's pause, rounds on* **Child** *with shocked expression*) Well I don't know where you heard language like that but if I ever hear anything like it again I'll wash your mouth out with soap and water. Now be quiet! (*To listener*) I'm sorry, I don't know where they get it from – I blame the teachers. He's just showing off really. Yes, I suppose we were all young once, you forget, don't you . . .

Child But Daddy, there's a fire!

Father Now look, we haven't got time for silly games.

Child But there really is a fire.

Father Look, important things like fires, Daddy knows about, right? So there isn't a fire!

Child (*Almost to self*) I think I know what a fire looks like.

Father (*Cross*) Do you want a smack?

Child (*Shakes head, sad expression*) No.

Father Well you're behaving as if you do! (*To listener*) Oh yes, well . . . you know. Keeping well. The what? . . . The operation? No – never had it in the end. And you? That's all cleared up has it? Because that was a bit of a worry wasn't it? But – oh no – not as bad as that, of course . . . (etc.)

Child But Daddy, there really is a fire!

Father	Right, any more of that and you're straight upstairs to bed.
Child	I don't think there'll be an upstairs.
Father	Right, that's it!
Child	Yes, I think it might be actually.
Father	Now that's enough! I've told you; important things like fires, Daddy knows about. So, there isn't a fire . . . you're much too young to . . . (*Sniffs air*) Can you smell that?
Child	(*Shakes head*) No.
Father	Can't you? Something's burning, I'm sure.
Child	Can't be, Daddy, 'cos you said there isn't a fire!
Father	(*Flustered*) What! Well – look! . . . look over there! (*Becoming louder*) There are flames and there's smoke! There is a fire! Fire! Fire! (*Running round in small circles*) Come on, get outside. Trust your mother to be out doing the weekly shop at a time like this. She just doesn't think.

END

It's easy to be like Dad: too busy and full of our own importance to listen to what others are trying to tell us, especially if they are younger than us or we feel them to be 'beneath' us in some other way. The next time someone has some advice or something else to offer, don't be too proud to accept it. For who are we to say whom God may choose to speak through?

A Cup of Tea

When we think of mission, we can often think we mean something very special and we can run away with the idea that it needs to be large, impressive, glamorous even. But the mission of taking God's love to others can take the form of simple acts of service for those who literally live next door; acts which can be performed by any of us at any time . . . anywhere. Pity nobody told Colonel Blithering Idiot . . .

Characters   Colonel Blithering Idiot: a pompous officer of the 'Old Guard'.
Sgt. Jones: an enthusiastic younger soldier.

(*The stage is empty. Enter, through the audience,* **Sgt. Jones,** *an enthusiastic, military-minded soldier. He performs some body rolls and similar 'combat' moves.* **Colonel Blithering Idiot** (*a much older man*) *makes a simultaneous but much slower entrance, perhaps from the opposite side of the room. The* **Colonel** *could attempt a roll but not really manage*)

Jones   Hut! Hut! Hut! (*As many times as necessary*)

Colonel   Hut! . . . Hut! . . . Cough . . . Splutter . . . Hut! . . . Wheeze.

(**Jones** *reaches the stage and there is a point at which he waits eagerly for the advance. The* **Colonel** *eventually joins him.* **Jones** *is champing at the bit*)

Jones   Shall I go in then, sir?

Colonel   Wait a minute, Jones. We've got to get ourselves all prepared. Remember the motto: 'If a job's worth doing . . .'

Jones   'It's worth letting everyone know you're doing it.'

Colonel	That's right, Jones. Right then, to make a real impression; first things first. Now we're at the house, have you got the plans?

(They both turn to face the audience)

Jones	The plans of the house, sir?
Colonel	No, Jones! The plans for the mission. Our glorious mission!
Jones	Oh those plans, sir, yes sir!
Colonel	Well, read them out, Jones, read them out.
Jones	Right, sir. Well, it concerns a Mr Evans, who is 76 years old, sir, and he's not been too well. He has in fact just come out of hospital after a minor operation. He can't get about too easily and he needs a bit of support.
Colonel	Exactly, Jones. And I'm sure we know exactly the sort of thing he'll need. And we're the very people to do it – the Crack Organisation For Emergencies!
Jones	The C OF E Sir!
Colonel	Yes, Jones, the C OF E, precisely! It takes a special unit like ourselves to deal with such a task as this, if it's to be done properly . . . nothing half-hearted. We know how to make sure that everybody knows we're busily involved in a mission. Now, Jones, have we got everything?
Jones	I think so, sir.
Colonel	Think so, Jones! Think so! Let's check it through man. Have we got the flares? *(The two are quite close together on stage, sitting or standing)*
Jones	They're not army issue any more, much tighter around the ankle.

Colonel	Not those sort of flares, Jones! Flares, you know, those things that light up the whole sky. Everybody will know what we're up to.
Jones	Well, we have got some, sir, but do you think they'll really be necessary?
Colonel	Of course they will be, Jones. People expect a mission to be dramatic. Now, have you got the abseiling ropes?
Jones	Well, yes, sir, but . . .
Colonel	Good. You're going to need those to get into the house. Crash through the first-storey window, then abseil your way down into the hall.
Jones	But couldn't we just knock on the door, sir?
Colonel	Knock on the door? Knock on the door? We're not the bally postman, Jones – we're an elite, crack unit.
Jones	I see, and once I'm inside, what should I do then?
Colonel	Well, I would have thought that was obvious, Jones. Something dramatic. Something large . . . and preferably very loud! Remember the motto, 'If a job's worth doing it's worth letting everybody know you're doing it'.
Jones	But shouldn't I ask Mr Evans what he wants, what he needs?
Colonel	Don't be so ridiculous, Jones. How on earth would he know what he wants – or needs? That's our job. We're bound to know best. We're an elite unit and we are doing this mission for goodness' sake! Now, when you're ready, at the word of command, after a count of three . . . One . . . (**Jones** *moves into a crouching position*) Two . . . (**Jones** *is poised on one foot and his hands. Something that looks fairly uncomfortable but which can be held for a while*)

You know, seeing you there like that Jones reminds me of the time when I was a young soldier myself. Not much older than you I shouldn't wonder. That would have been back in nineteen thirty . . . three.

Jones   Three, sir. Here I go! (*He dashes off*)

Colonel   (*Continues rambling. Can ad lib if preferred*) Yes, back then when I'd just got my first stripes, young Ginger Jenkins and I used to get up to all sorts of jolly japes and get ourselves into the most awful scrapes. Oh, we had a lot of laughs back in those days. Don't see much of Ginger these days but we had good times back then. I remember one particular Sergeant Major. Terrifying fella. Giant of a man. Huge, bristling moustache. Served under Kitchener apparently, and he was, to put it bluntly, Jones, a downright bully of the highest order! Anyway, he had it in for Ginger and me, so we vowed that we would somehow take him down a peg or two. And I'll tell you what, Jones, I still remember the look on his face when he came out onto the parade ground and there, fluttering from the flagpole for all the world to see, was a large pair of his wife's . . .

Jones   (*Interrupting, having returned*) Excuse me, sir.

Colonel   (*Taken a little by surprise*) What, Jones . . . mission accomplished then? Surely not?

Jones   Er . . . yes, sir.

Colonel   (*Confused*) How can it be, Jones? I didn't see any flares or hear any very loud noises.

Jones   There was no need, sir.

Colonel   No need! Of course there's a need: we're on a mission, Jones, and we want people to know it! Now stop messing about and go in there and sort out Mr Evans properly.

Jones	Well sir, I already have.
Colonel	(*Blustering*) Already have! What on earth do you mean? You haven't carried out any of the things we had planned for him yet!
Jones	Well actually, sir, I asked him what he wanted and he just wanted me to make him a cup of tea because he finds it difficult getting to the kitchen and back.
Colonel	(*In disbelief*) A cup of tea?
Jones	Yes, sir . . . and he wanted a biscuit.
Colonel	A biscuit?
Jones	(*Hesitantly*) A . . . custard cream, sir.
Colonel	I don't care if it was a Fortnum and Mason macaroon, Jones! The fact is that we came here to perform a mission. A mission that we had carefully planned and where we knew exactly what we were going to do. We knew what was needed here, Jones, because we are a crack unit. The Crack Organisation for Emergencies!
Jones	The C OF E Sir.
Colonel	Yes, the C OF E, Jones. I don't go marching up and down all over Dartmoor with a huge 100 pound haversack on my back, sleeping in a bracken shelter, eating gorse and berries for weeks on end, just to go into someone's house to make them a cup of tea and to get them a biscuit!
	(*They begin to move off*)
Jones	But it's what Mr Evans needed, sir. It's what he wanted.

Colonel	I don't care what he thinks he needs or what he thinks he wants, Jones. I had come to do a mission. Where was the drama? Where was the action? Where were the very loud noises? Nowhere! 'If a job's worth doing, it's worth letting everybody know you're doing it!' It's not on, Jones!
Jones	No, sir!
Colonel	It's just not on!
Jones	No, sir!
Colonel	Will you stop saying 'No, sir'.
Jones	Yes, sir.
Colonel	Jones!
Jones	Yes, sir?
Colonel	Be quiet!
Jones	Yes, sir.
Colonel	Jones, will you be quiet!
Jones	Yes, sir.
Colonel	Jones!

(*Exit still carrying on in this fashion.*)

END

Colonel Blithering Idiot's glorious mission, gloriously missed the point. Sgt. Jones, meanwhile, just got on with what needed to be done. It's easy to use the excuse that mission needs to be a dramatic affair to be worthwhile and if it isn't, there's no point doing it. But effective mission is about simply responding to the needs of others, and that can have a dramatic effect, even without the drama!

The Famous Two Go Hiking

Being a child must be so frustrating. Everybody seems to know what's best for you, especially parents: What you should do, what you shouldn't do, when you should, when you shouldn't . . .

Why can't they leave you alone and stop poking their noses in? Surely they don't always know what's best? What you can cope with on your own and when you need help? Do they really know just what you can handle or are they being an old stick-in-the-mud?

Perhaps . . . and then, perhaps not!

Characters	Jeremy: a self-confident boy. A pupil of the 'Enid Blyton School of Life'.
	Timothy: Jeremy's sensible, younger brother, a pupil of the same school.
Tim	(*Energetically*) Oh, golly gosh – these summer hols are super!
Jeremy	I should say! We've had some spiffing adventures.
Tim	Yes, absolutely wizard fun.
Jeremy	Yes. And I'm glad Lucy our younger sister isn't with us.
Tim	Oh yes, Lu . . . She'd have been a real wet blanket. Why, I bet she's at home right now with Mummy . . . playing with her dollies.
Jeremy	(*Showing his disgust*) Dollies! Eugh . . . Pooey!
Tim	Yes, we wouldn't have been able to come half as far if Lucy had been with us.
Jeremy	Yes, that's the bother with having a younger sister.
Tim	Still, that long climb has made me hot. Would you like some ginger pop and cakes?
Jeremy	Oh whizzo! Yes, please!

Tim	(*Searching in his rucksack*) Oh dear. I seem to have forgotten them.
Jeremy	Oh, you silly sausage.
Tim	Oh, don't be so beastly – it's not my fault you know – I didn't do it on purpose.
Jeremy	Oh, never mind. Maybe there'll be some fizzy lemonade when we get across that. (*Pointing off-stage*)
Tim	(*Anxiously*) Across that? (*Looking off stage and pointing*)
Jeremy	Yes, across the swirly stream.
Tim	The swirly stream?
Jeremy	Yes, the splashy, swirly stream.
Tim	The splashy, swirly stream?
Jeremy	(*Dramatically*) Yes, the scary, splashy, swirly stream . . . come on, let's go!
Tim	No, I don't think we should!
Jeremy	Why ever not? It will be a wizard prank!
Tim	But Daddy said we should wait, and he'd help us!
Jeremy	Oh, don't be such a frightful bore!
Tim	I'm not! It's just that Daddy said he knows what's best for us and he'd find a safe way across.
Jeremy	Well, I'm going to find my own way.
Tim	But I think we should trust Daddy; he did say he'd help!
Jeremy	I don't care what Daddy says!
Tim	But Daddy says it could be dangerous if we try to do it all on our own.

Jeremy	Well, I think Daddy's an old stick-in-the-mud.
Tim	I'm jolly well going to tell him you said that!
Jeremy	I don't care. You can jolly well go and tell him I said it. Why, we have much more fun than this in my dorm at Big School. We have pillow fights and midnight feasts and . . .
Tim	(*Interrupting*) Yes, but you seem to forget . . . I'm not at Big School yet!
Jeremy	Yes . . . that's just the bother with having a younger brother.
Tim	But I'll be coming up to Big School soon!
Jeremy	Yes, and if you behave like this I'll have nothing to do with you! I don't want my chums thinking I've got a girl for a brother! Why, you'll probably be playing with Lu's dollies next!
Together	(*Again showing suitable disgust*) Dollies! Eugh . . . Pooey!
Jeremy	Come on, let's go!
Tim	No, we mustn't!
Jeremy	(*Jeering*) I just think you're scared. Scaredy cat, scaredy cat, sitting on a door mat!
Tim	(*Upset*) Oh, you can be frightfully beastly at times!
Jeremy	(*Defiantly*) Well, I'm going anyway! And there's probably lashings of fizzy lemonade on the other side and I'm going to drink it all myself! Goodbye! (*Exits*)
Tim	(*To himself*) Hope it makes you sick. I don't think we should go . . .
	(*We hear pitifully soggy screaming from* Jeremy, *off stage*)

Tim	(*Calling to* **Jeremy**) Oh gosh, what's the matter?
Jeremy	I've gone and fallen right in! That's the matter.
Tim	Oh dear, you got a bit of a soaking! Serves you right! So, Daddy did know what was best for us after all. (*Pause. Then with an air of 'I told you so'*) Oh look . . . here he comes now.
Jeremy	(*Sarcastically*) Oh, good!
Tim	Yes, and he's bringing his boat so we can get across safely and keep nice and dry!
Jeremy	Oh, good.
Tim	You see, I told you we should have listened to Daddy.
Jeremy	Oh, shut up!
Tim	But if you'd waited for Da . . .
Jeremy	Shut up!
Tim	But if you'd listened, then Daddy would have . . .
Jeremy	Shut up!
Tim	Well if you're going to speak to me like that and be such a rotten stinker, I'll just leave you to it! Goodbye! (*He exits.*)
Jeremy	(*His calls becoming more pitiful*) Um . . . Timmy, um . . . Timmy . . . I didn't mean it . . . don't go . . . Oh Timmy!

END

God, our Heavenly Father, often gives us very clear instructions about what we should be doing, giving us help and guidance to get through many situations. Perhaps we think we can cope on our own? Perhaps we think God's way is boring . . . not for us?

But if we ignore him, we invariably finish 'up to our necks in it'!

Mission to Pontefract

We sometimes think that we know just the best way to share the Gospel. All you have to do is tailor it to suit the specific needs of the individual. If you know what makes them tick, you can make your Gospel relevant and everything will be spot on. But what does make people tick? From a distance we may think we know the answer.

Meet Giles and Julian. They have put an awful lot of effort into finding out about their intended recipients (or should that say victims?) All from over 200 miles away – very commendable!

Really?

Characters   Julian: upper crust, patronising, totally out of touch.
Giles: upper crust, patronising, totally out of touch.

(Julian and Giles on stage. They are discussing a proposed visit to the North of England. They have very exaggerated 'posh' southern accents)

Julian   Well I must say, Giles, I'm really looking forward to our mission to Pontefract.

Giles   Oh yes, I think there's so much that we have to offer.

Julian   But I think it's important that we remember that they're not quite like us.

Giles   Oh no . . . there's lots of differences. I mean, the clothes for a start. I mean, if we turned up dressed like this, we'd stick out like a sore thumb.

Julian   Oh yes, of course.

Giles   You know they all wear cloth caps.

Julian   I didn't know that! And the women too?

Giles	Oh yes, and the clogs as well. So we're going to need some of those for our mission.
Julian	Well, I've been doing a bit of research of my own and I've discovered that they don't really speak the same as us and if we're going to really make contact with these people we're going to have to speak in a language they understand. And so to help us in this I've jotted down a few useful phrases. Here's one . . . (*Shows notebook*)
Giles	Oh, do let me see. Now then, right . . . What's this one here . . . 'E L O'.
Julian	Well actually it's more like this . . . (*In an exaggerated northern accent*) 'Eee 'ello'.
Giles	(*Trying it again*) 'Eee 'ello.' Yes I see . . . And when would one use that?
Julian	Well, it's . . . it's a form of greeting really.
Giles	Mm, mm, yes, I see. Well that one will be very useful then, when we first arrive, for example. I'm sure we'll really make an impact if we use that. I see you've got another one there . . . (*Again saying it as it is written*) 'Way lad . . . Way lad.'
Julian	Well, actually it's 'Waaay Lad'. Much more emphasis on the 'a' . . . it's very drawn out.
Giles	'Waay lad', 'waay lad' . . . Right I see . . . and when would one use that?
Julian	Well, again it's one of those rather tricky things that doesn't translate exactly into our own . . . er . . . language as it were, but I suppose it roughly means, um . . . 'Oh come off it, old chap'. But you can also say it with a little lighter touch on the 'Waay', so more like 'Way lad', and in this instance it would be more of a casual greeting.

Giles   Oh gosh, I see. So it's got more than one meaning, depending on how it's said. Quite a complex language code then?

Julian   Oh, yes.

Giles   Well, like you, I've had a thought or two about how we might deliver our message to the people of Pontefract. And what I think will help is this. I think if we make just a few slight changes to some of the words of the Gospels, I feel it will help to make them just a touch more relevant to them. For example, I thought of something like . . . (*Exaggerated northern accent*) 'The Lord loves you and he loves your whippet'.

Julian   Oh yes . . . That's very good . . . I think they'll respond to that.

Giles   And (*Exaggerated northern accent*) 'Which of you fathers, if your son asks for an Eccles cake, would give him a snake instead?'

Julian   (*Taking up the theme. Exaggerated northern accent*) 'Or if he asks for black pudding, will give him a scorpion?' Yes, they're very good. I'm sure we really are going to speak to the people of Pontefract with things like that.

Giles   Also I thought (*Exaggerated northern accent*) 'Consider the tatties in the field. They do not labour or spin. Yet I tell you not even Solomon in all his splendour was dressed like one of these.'

Julian   Oh yes, and what about (*Exaggerated northern accent*) 'And not one racing pigeon falls t' ground apart from the will of your Father.'

Giles   And I think perhaps, (*Exaggerated northern accent*) 'Every hair under your cloth cap is counted.'

Julian   Well I think all those are going to be very successful.

Giles I think music will play an important role too.

Julian Oh yes, I hear that this is a very popular tune (*Hums a bit of Dvořák's Symphony No. 9; i.e. the Hovis advert tune*)

Giles Oh yes, I know it. Perhaps we could fit some words to the tune. Like 'Onward Christian Soldiers'.

  (They both sing 'Onward Christian soldiers, marching as to war', making the words fit with ridiculously extended vowel sounds where necessary)

Giles Oh yes, that's perfect. Well I really am looking forward to our mission to Pontefract.

Julian I think we're really going to make a long-lasting impression.

  (*Exit humming Hovis advert*)

END

It is certain that Giles and Julian would have made a big impression on the good people of Pontefract. The memories of their visit would have lasted a very long time indeed. But what they had to say would, with equal certainty, have been quickly forgotten, hidden as it was beneath their pointless pretence at empathy.

The way to be relevant is to be real with people and to get to know them. It is about relationships – not our ideas, conceived at a distance.

Towering Troubles

From instant coffee to instant cameras, everything needs to be done immediately. But with important things, really important things, shouldn't we take a little more time? If a job's worth doing, it's worth doing well!

Well, I'm not sure Brother Lorenzo down at the monastery would agree . . .

Characters   Brother Lorenzo: an Italian monk – young, energetic but naive and eager for results.
Brother Francesco: an Italian monk, level-headed with sound advice.

(*Brother Lorenzo is up a ladder or raised above ground level in some other way. He is hammering. Enter Brother Francesco*)

BF   (*Calling out and up. Trying to be heard above the hammering*) Brother Lorenzo!

BL   Eh?

BF   Brother Lorenzo, stop your hammering!

BL   I can't hear you, I'm hammering!

BF   I know you are hammering . . . that is why I am asking you to stop your hammering!

BL   Hang on Brother Francesco, I will stop my hammering . . . (*He stops*) Now, what were you saying?

BF   I was asking you to stop hammering.

BL   But I have stopped hammering.

BF   I know you have stopped hammering.

BL   (*A little confused*) But if I have stopped hammering why are you asking me to stop hammering?

BF   (*Not wishing to be drawn into an argument, so with restrained anger*) I am asking you to stop hammering so that I can ask you what it is you do.

BL   (*Proudly*) Why, I am building a wonderful tall tower that will bring great honour to our monastery.

BF   A wonderful tall tower! (*There is a hint of doubt in his voice*) That is good . . . but (*He looks doubtfully around him*) But here, Lorenzo? Isn't this patch of ground rather damp and soggy? Surely you need somewhere dry?

BL   (*Unperturbed by this question*) No, it will be fine, you'll see.

BF   (*Not convinced*) So you say, but . . . I don't know.

(**Brother Lorenzo** *returns to work, this time sawing*)

BF   (*Calling above the noise*) Brother Lorenzo!

BL   Eh?

BF   Brother Lorenzo stop your sawing!

BL   I can't hear you Brother Francesco . . . I'm sawing.

BF   I know you are sawing . . . that is why I am asking you to stop sawing.

BL   Hang on, Brother Francesco, I'll stop sawing. (*He stops*) Now what is it you are saying?

BF   I was asking you to stop sawing.

BL   But I have stopped sawing.

BF   (*Exasperated*) I know you have stopped sawing!

BL   (*Confused*) But if I have stopped sawing why have you asked me to stop sawing?

BF   (*Desperately trying to control his temper*) I am asking you to stop . . . (*Brief pause and then more calmly*) Never mind. Brother Lorenzo, a big, tall tower such as this will take many years to complete, no?

BL   (*Confidently*) No . . . coupla days.

BF   A couple of days! Couple of days! No, no. (*Shaking head*) No, you will not live to see its completion. And the novices we have in the monastery now will not see its completion. (*Warming to his theme*) And the novices who are not yet novices but who will be novices when the novices who are novices now are no longer novices, will not see its completion. And the novices who . . .

BL   Brother Francesco!

BF   Eh?

BL   Shut up. Coupla days I tell you and it will be, magnifico!

BF   (*Still not convinced*) So you say but . . . I don't know.

     (*Brother Lorenzo returns to his work*)

BF   (*Calling up*) Brother Lorenzo!

BL   Eh?

BF   Brother Lorenzo, where is all the gold and silver and precious jewels?

BL   What gold and silver and precious jewels?

BF   The gold, silver and precious jewels you are using to make this tower truly magnificent.

BL   But I'm not using gold or silver or precious jewels.

BF   (*In disbelief*) You're not using any gold or silver or precious jewels?

BL   (*Cutting across him impatiently*) No, I'm not using any gold or silver or precious jewels!

BF   Then, what are you using?

BL   (*Matter-of-factly*) Wood.

BF   (*Approvingly*) Ah . . . fine Brazilian mahogany, many patterned rosewoods and mighty oaken beams.

BL   No . . . (*Almost embarrassed, defensive*) a bit of ply.

BF   (*Incredulous*) A bit of ply! A bit of ply! You are using a bit of plywood?

BL   Yes! Think of all the money I've saved. And, of course, it will be so much quicker! Not such hard work. (*Pause*) Brother Francesco, pass me up some nails.

BF   But I can't see any nails.

BL   Yes, down there on the floor.

BF   (*Bending down*) But these are rusty and bent; they will be no good.

BL   They will be fine. (*Some are passed up*) And some more.

BF   There are no more.

BL   I will come down. I'm sure I can find something to hold up the work I've done. (*Comes down. Both stand looking admiringly. During the next speech, after 'proud the tower is', both begin to slowly bend sideways, as if watching the slow and steady collapse of the tower*) See, look. See how tall and proud the tower is. How very . . . very . . . um . . . how very . . . um . . . oh! What a mighty fall that was!

BF	(*They begin to exit slowly part-way through this speech*) Yes. Why the novices will not have seen a fall like that. And the novices who are not yet novices but who will be novices when the novices who are now novices . . .
BL	Brother Francesco!
BF	Eh?
BL	Shut up!

END

Some things don't just happen overnight. They need planning, care, wisdom and prayer. In short, they need firm foundations. Building our Christian life needs all this and much more. And if it really is to be honouring to God, what are we building it with? Things of worth and value that bring honour, or things that are pretty flimsy at the best of times? Because when things are put to the test – and they will be – will they stand or will they . . .

Oops!

Heaven's Above

Everyone seems to have an idea about what heaven is like, from angels with harps on whiter-than-white clouds, to a sandy beach where the sun always shines and there's free cocktails for everyone. From the sublime to the ridiculous.

For some, spending a lifetime with someone may seem like heaven but then if they're anything like Jasmine, it may not. But don't tell Rupert.

Is this really what heaven's all about?

Characters Rupert: a dashing young chap of the 'Roaring '20s'. Jasmine: his fiancée; an innocent young thing, besotted with Rupert.

(*Rupert and Jasmine are seated looking affectionately at one another*)

Rupert Darling . . . I must go.

Jasmine Oh, don't say that, Rupert . . . you mustn't.

Rupert (*Gently insistent*) But darling, I must.

Jasmine (*Anguished*) Oh no, Rupert, no!

Rupert But darling, I must go. (*We become aware by his actions that* **Rupert** *needs to visit the lavatory.* **Jasmine** *is not so quick on the uptake*)

Jasmine But why, Rupert? Why?

Rupert Darling . . . I'm desperate to go!

Jasmine (*Understanding at last*) Oh I see . . . but you will come back? You won't leave without me?

Rupert No, darling . . . (*not seeing how this is possible*) you've got the car keys in your bag.

Jasmine	No . . . No . . . I mean, you will come back, you will come back to me?
Rupert	Well yes, I live here.
Jasmine	I know, Rupert, but you'll always come back to me?
Rupert	Oh yes, I'll always come back to you, Jasmine.
Jasmine	Oh Rupert, you know, tonight I feel that there's a special atmosphere, a special electricity in the air. Do you think it could be the champagne talking?
Rupert	Oh no, not the champagne . . . but our love, our hearts beating . . . our passion, one for the other.
Jasmine	Oh, do you really think so, Rupert?
Rupert	Oh, yes, my poppet.
Jasmine	Oh, I love it when you call me your poppet.
Rupert	(*Affectionately*) Do you? (*Pause*) You know, tonight, when we're together like this . . . I know heaven will be like this.
Jasmine	Do you really think so? Do you really think heaven will be like this?
Rupert	Oh yes, just like this. Bound to be!
Jasmine	(*Having some concerns*) But will we have a new settee?
Rupert	Oh yes, of course. A very big one – that's what heaven's all about. Us, having all the luxuries we want, for ever and ever.
Jasmine	And will there be champagne?
Rupert	Oh yes, oceans of champagne.
Jasmine	And gin?

Rupert	Rivers of gin!
Jasmine	And Cinzano?
Rupert	Lakes of Cinzano!
Jasmine	And claret?
Rupert	Yes.
Jasmine	And sherry?
Rupert	(*Tiring*) Yes, dear, I think all your favourite drinks will be there.
Jasmine	And will there be coconut?
Rupert	Sure to be, darling.
Jasmine	(*Disappointed*) But I don't like coconut!
Rupert	Then I shall make sure there isn't any!
Jasmine	Can you really do that?
Rupert	Well, if a fella can't fix it so there's no coconut for his girl, what sort of a heaven would it be? That's not my idea of heaven, let me tell you!
Jasmine	Oh Rupert, you're so wonderful . . . I don't believe all those things Mummy says about you.
Rupert	(*Slightly concerned*) Er . . . what things?
Jasmine	Oh nothing.
Rupert	No, what?
Jasmine	(*Hesitantly*) Well . . . (*Then quite quickly*) just that you're a cad and a bounder and an awful gold digger and not to be trusted . . . but I don't believe that.

Rupert   (*Looking and sounding a little uncomfortable*) No, Jasmine, no you mustn't. Just remember we'll always be together and you'll always be my angel.

Jasmine   Oh, Rupert, you say the loveliest things. (*Pause*) Rupert, have you ever called anyone 'your angel' before?

Rupert   (*On dodgy ground*) Oh no, (*Deciding honesty is the best policy*) . . . well . . . just Milly.

Jasmine   (*Disappointed*) Oh.

Rupert   And Molly . . .

Jasmine   (*A little anxious*) Oh.

Rupert   Oh, and Mandy.

Jasmine   (*Exasperated*) Milly, Molly and Mandy?

Rupert   Yes, but only once . . . and I was probably drunk at the time.

Jasmine   Oh Rupert, but you're not drunk now?

Rupert   Only with my love for you, my dear! Remember, we'll always be together, now – and then, for ever and ever in heaven, with all the things we've ever wanted. (*Pause. A clasp of her hand perhaps.* **Rupert** *remembers his earlier problem*) But Jasmine, as I said, I really do need to go.

Jasmine   But I thought you wanted to stay with me for ever?

Rupert   Yes I do, but I'm desperate to go.

Jasmine   But how can you go and stay? Can't I go with you?

Rupert   (*Firmly*) Definitely not, no. (*Patiently explaining*) I need to go. But then I'll be back.

Jasmine   Oh yes, I remember now. Oh, Rupert, I'm so looking forward to heaven.

Rupert   Yes darling, heaven will be just what we want it to be and we can do just whatever we choose. Goodbye my love. (*He exits*)

Jasmine   Goodbye, darling! (*Calling after him*) Missing you already!

END

Well if that's heaven, good luck to them. Often our images of heaven seem to revolve around us and our own personal wants and desires. We seem to forget what and who heaven is really all about. Heaven is not our plan for us, it's God's plan for us and therefore, surely, infinitely better.

Sheriff P. J. Brody Makes a Stand

Isn't it nice when everything's in order? No unnecessary complications. Everything just the way we want it. But what do we do in the times when it's not like that? Surely the important thing is to make sure nothing messes up our routines or our plans for the way things should be. Ain't that right? Well, just ask Sheriff P. J. Brody . . . he'll tell ya!

Characters P. J. Brody: a dedicated but misguided sheriff of the 'Old West'.

Jake: a conscientious and law-abiding citizen of the same town.

(**P. J. Brody** *is seated at a table, carefully polishing his Sheriff's badge. Suddenly* **Jake** *bursts in*)

Jake (*Excitedly*) Sheriff! Sheriff Brody! It's Texas Ted and his boys, they're a'ridin' this way! I just know there's gonna be trouble.

P.J. (*Casually*) With you in a moment, Jake.

Jake (*Extremely agitated*) But Sheriff Brody, they're headin' right this way!

P.J. (*He looks up from his task*) Now just hold onto your horses there, Jake. I'll be with you when I'm done here. (*Returning to his polishing*)

Jake (*Not quite believing this*) Sheriff! Ain't you listening? It's Texas Ted and his boys . . . they's wanted for robbery in five counties!

P.J. (*Still with no urgency*) Say, now that you're here . . . what d'ya think?

Jake (*Puzzled*) 'Bout what?

P.J.	'Bout my Sheriff's badge. (*He holds it up as if to catch the light*) Dog gonnit Jake, I've spent three hours polishing that. See the way it shines? A man could shave in that there star, Jake.
Jake	Sheriff, thing's is lookin' bad!
P.J.	You mean you don't think it's shiny?
Jake	(*Exasperated*) No, Sheriff, Texas Ted and his boys are comin' this way! The town needs your protection. What are ya gonna do?
P.J.	Well, there's ma spurs need shinin' . . . now I got that badge lookin' so good. A sheriff ain't no sheriff in my eyes till he's got himself some bright shinin' spurs.
Jake	(*Pleading but with a touch of anger*) Listen, Sheriff Brody, there's women and children in this town needs you.
P.J.	Well, I'm gonna need ma gun . . .
Jake	(*Relieved at last to have got somewhere*) Great! You're gonna go out there and fight 'em!
P.J.	Let me finish . . . I'm gonna need ma gun . . . clean. Wadda folks gonna think of me with a dirty gun in ma holster?
Jake	(*Resigned*) Oh I give up! (*Exits*)
P.J.	Well now . . . if I can just get some polish on these boots . . . a sheriff's no good to no one if he looks all messed up. Gotta take a pride in what ya doin' . . . too few folks take any pride these days . . . no wonder the West's the way it is . . .
	(**Jake** *returns*)
Jake	(*Matter of factly*) Er, Sheriff . . . No need to worry about Texas Ted and his boys . . . they've gone.

THE LOG IN MY EYE

P.J.   (*With a touch of 'I told you there was nothing to worry about'*) Yeah? . . . Great news, Jake.

Jake   Yep, they've gone . . . along with all the money from the bank and the saloon, five ladies' jewellery, old Nathaniel's gold, seven horses, fifty head of cattle, seventy sheep, the church bells, a piano, Ma Goodman's rockin' chair, Ma Goodman, my guitar, ten barrels of whisky, your daughter's new puppy dog, the stage coach, a set of champagne glasses . . .

P.J.   (*Cutting in*) They didn't take ma broom did they? I still gotta get ma Sheriff's office lookin' spic and span. If they've taken that broom I don't know what I'm gonna do . . . Come on, Jake, stop your yabberin', boy . . . We got a broom to find!

(*They exit*)

END

Sheriff P. J. Brody had it all worked out. Nothing could sway him from what he thought was important. Nothing could make him change his plans or his priorities. And what did he do when he was really needed? Nothing! Sometimes we need to forego the comfort of following our plans . . . doing things our way. We need to be ready to respond to all situations in an effective way – whether it's what we planned or not.

Three O'Clock and All's Well

'Why oh why can't people listen?'

'Pardon?'

'I said, why oh why can't . . . oh never mind!'

Some of us are great listeners. We have no problem in that area. It's just other people who do. Isn't that right?

Characters   A. Moaner Esq.: a self-righteous person.

Nightwatchman: modelled on an Olde Worlde caricature.

(**A. Moaner Esq.** *appears on the stage and begins to address the audience, as if having a bit of a moan to a friend. Almost as soon as he starts, the* **Nightwatchman** *enters with much coughing and spluttering. He delivers his line ('Three o'clock and all's well!') in the manner of a nightwatchman from the days of old. This is punctuated by over-emphasised, terrible coughing . . . anything to draw attention to himself*)

A. Moaner   Well, I'll tell you that the problem in the church today – in my opinion – is that people just don't listen. Oh, they may think they do but as far as I'm concerned they don't.

Night-watchman   Three o'clock and all's well!

A. Moaner   Certainly not in my experience anyway. Now, I'm not one to complain but I do find it very difficult when people can't be bothered to make the effort to listen. I'm as ready as the next to sit down and hear what people have to say but it seems to me as if I'm part of a dying breed.

Night-watchman	Three o'clock and all's well!
A. Moaner	You know the old adage – we have one mouth and two ears – we need to do twice the amount of listening as we do speaking. Yes, some say it's a skill but I think if we're to get anywhere in the church today we must learn to listen. We must unblock those ears, 'pin back those lugholes', as they say, or we will miss out on something very important.
Night-watchman	Three o'clock and all's well!
A. Moaner	You know, you try everything to get people along to a simple meeting. You can tell them about that meeting until you're blue in the face, stick announcements on the notice board, write it in the newsletter and remind them again and again, but do they come? No! They say they didn't know anything about it. And why? Because they simply don't listen . . .
Night-watchman	Three o'clock and all's well!
A. Moaner	Anyway, must dash – (*to the* **Nightwatchman**) I say, you don't happen to have the time do you?

END

Good communication is the key to successful relationships between individuals and within the church. No matter how good we think we are at communicating, most of us have much more practice at speaking than we do at listening. Do we really listen effectively or are we much more concerned about what we have to say?

Advent Calendars 'R' Us

Christmas comes but once a year and when it does it brings . . . turkey and presents and wine and mince pies and chocolates and chestnuts (roasted on an open fire) and . . . and . . . What was that other thing Christmas was about . . .?

Even as Christians or as a church, we can sometimes all too easily get sidetracked – but surely never as badly as the employees of Advent Calendars 'R' Us?

Characters   A.J.: The Managing Director of 'Advent Calendars 'R' Us'. A rather pompous, 'old-school-tie' sort of chap.
Millard: An eager and somewhat fawning underling from the design department.

A.J. is seated at a table. He becomes aware of Millard waiting to enter.

A.J.   Ah . . . Millard. Come in. Come and sit down. *(Millard enters and sits)* I understand you have some interesting, innovative ideas for our next Advent calendar?

Millard   Oh yes, A.J.! Certainly. I'm very excited about it.

A.J.   Excited, eh?

Millard   Oh yes, very excited.

A.J.   Jolly good, jolly good. *(Pause)* Well, Millard, don't keep me in suspense!

Millard   Oh yes, certainly, A.J. . . . Well, you know Advent calendars . . . ?

A.J.   Yes, Millard. As managing director of 'Advent Calendars 'R' Us Limited', I think it's fair to say that I do know about Advent calendars . . . so don't waste my time.

Millard (*Apologetically*) Oh yes, certainly, A.J. Well, as you know, there are many sorts of Advent calendars. Those with chocolates in, some with novelty toys . . . some with 3D pictures. Well, what we've come up with, A.J., is this . . . (*Holds out ordinary-looking Advent calendar*)

A.J. It looks like a perfectly ordinary Advent calendar to me, Millard.

Millard It might look like it, A.J. . . . but honestly, it's not!

A.J. (*Unconvinced*) Well, what makes it so different then?

Millard It's 'scratch and sniff', A.J.!

A.J. 'Scratch and sniff' you say? Really?

Millard (*Becoming even more enthusiastic*) Yes, yes, it is! You open the door with the number on . . . see, here's door number one. (*Leans over to show A.J. the correct door*) And look, behind the door there's a picture . . . a plate of Christmassy mince pies. See? And then you scratch that little bit there at the top of the picture and sniff. Have a go, A.J.!

A.J. Scratch there, you say? And sniff? (*He scratches, then takes a good sniff. He is surprised and pleased with the result*) Well I never! You know it does! It smells just like a plate of mince pies! Yes, very clever . . . and, if I'm not mistaken there's a hint of brandy butter there.

Millard Yes, yes! Well spotted, A.J.!

A.J. (*Without thinking*) I think I know the smell of brandy well enough, Millard. (*Realises what he has said and coughs to cover up*) Um . . . Right! . . . Jolly good. Now then, what else have you got there?

Millard (*Still enthusiastic*) Well, under door number 11, we have a Christmas tree. You try that one, A.J.

A.J. (*He opens the small door, scratches and sniffs*) Mmm! That's lovely. Pine needles. Smells just like a

Norwegian forest! I think we're on to a winner here, Millard!

Millard Oh yes, we searched about for ideas for the pictures and we've used some of the traditional Christmas songs. Here's a good example. Tell you what, A.J., why not close your eyes and have a sniff and see if you can guess what it is?

A.J. Hmm. Sounds fun! Why not? (*He shuts his eyes*) OK, my eyes are shut. You'll have to scratch the picture for me, of course.

Millard Righto! (*He scratches the picture on the calendar*) Ready. Sniff away, A.J.

A.J. (*Sniffs and recoils slightly*) Ugh! Can't say I like that, Millard. To be honest it smells like the wrong end of a cow.

Millard Well, actually A.J., you're almost right. It's from that song . . . you know, 'The twelve days of Christmas'? It's the seven maids a-milking. Have a look, A.J.

A.J. (*Opens his eyes and looks at the calendar*) Oh yes, there they are with their cows. Marvellous! This is wonderful, Millard. I think this is just the break-through 'Advent Calendars 'R' Us Limited' is after.

Millard (*Hesitantly*) Yes, yes, um. But we do have a bit of a problem.

A.J. I see . . . bit of a sting in the tail is there, Millard? What's the matter? You're not going to tell me those smells are poisonous, are you?

Millard Oh no, nothing as drastic as that.

A.J. Well, I can't see what the matter is. It all looks fine to me. I mean, you've even got the double doors for number 24, and it's right in the middle of the calendar. Best place for it. The big finale! So come on, let's see what's behind those doors.

Millard Well that's just it, A.J., that's the problem. We haven't got a picture for number 24 . . . Christmas Eve!

A.J.	What? No picture? Got to have a picture for Number 24. Most important part of it!
Millard	Oh yes, I know that, A.J. That's why we're in a bit of a quandary. We've been racking our brains for something really relevant. We've had our top creative people on it.
A.J.	And drawn a blank, eh?
Millard	So far.
A.J.	Have you asked around?
Millard	Well yes, and that's when someone said Wilkins down in despatches had said something about a baby. Adamant about there being something to do with Christmas and a baby.
A.J.	A baby? A baby? Something to do with Christmas? I don't think so. Don't see the relevance myself, do you, Millard?
Millard	Well I must say, A.J., I was at a bit of a loss myself.
A.J.	Couldn't you have a picture of a big Christmas pudding, covered in brandy, bottle of port beside it? You know, a nice festive scene? A bit of good food and all that. I means that's what Christmas is all about, isn't it?
Millard	Oh yes, quite right. Absolutely, A.J.!

(They exit)

END

It's easy for us to say just how special Christmas is, but it's also very easy to forget why, as we get caught up in all the busy-ness and tradition. Christmas is special because it is about the birth of Jesus Christ, the Saviour of the World. A simple statement but a monumental fact!

The Prayer of Crucifixion

'Hands together and eyes closed.' Prayer can become a bit of a ritual . . . a routine. But what do we really think about when we pray? What would be revealed if someone could actually hear what went on in our heads as we prayed? It's a scary thought . . . because, you know, someone can!

Characters   Figure: A lone figure who is ready to pray.
                              Christ.

                              (The figure moves on to the stage and assumes an attitude of prayer)

Figure   *(Genuine contrition)* Dear Lord, I'm sorry for all the things I've done to let you down, in particular I'm sorry for the way I responded to Phil and in future I will try to be more tolerant. I know that's what you want from me. But it's not easy.

                              *(From this point we see the crucifixion acted out behind the speaker. We see a lone figure representing **Christ** who acts out a simple crucifixion scene which is appropriately timed to finish with the **Figure**'s line 'It's just not fair'. The crucifixion scene is done through mime so there is no sound to detract from the voice of the praying figure. The scene may be simply enacted by using a small stepladder to elevate **Christ** on the cross)*

                              (Having lost the contrition) In fact, try as I might not to, sometimes I almost think he deserves it. He can be so unthinking. And here I am saying sorry. When I think about it, it ought really to be him apologising, not me! I mean he's the one who said all those things in the first place. Like I say, he just doesn't think. Actually, the whole way he goes

about things is really hurtful to me and I'm the one who suffers. I don't think he realises the pain he causes me. This is the wrong way round. It's him who's wrong, not me!

(*With growing feeling*) You know, when I think about it, it always seems to be me doing things for other people. Always! No one ever seems to do anything for me. I'm always the one who takes the brunt of things, the rough end, all the unpleasantness. I'm the one who ends up paying the price for others. I'd like to see someone putting that sort of effort in on my account, but it doesn't happen. It just isn't fair!

Christ   It is finished! (**Christ** *dies*)

Figure   No, it just isn't fair!

END

Christ died for who and for what? Too often we forget. Let's pray we don't!